Coverup (the Visard)
---The Women of Our Lives---

By M.Weisgerber
(2007-2017)

--First Edition--

A CIP catalogue record for this title is available from the British Library.

Lexile Reading Level = 1385+

Library of Congress Cataloging in Publication Data

Weisgerber, Mark
    Coverup, The Visard (The Women of Our Lives) / by Mark Weisgerber

    Poetry to Important Women: p.86, 12.7cm x 20.32cm
    Excludes index.

    ISBN # 978-1-954339-03-3 (hardcover)
    ISBN # 978-1-954339-04-0 (paperback)
    ISBN # 978-1-954339-05-7 (ebook)

1. Love Poetry 2. Verse & Rhythms 3. Poems and sonnets 4. Michigan & DC— American Fiction & Non Fiction.

LCCN 2020923548 (paperback)
DDC 811.03   PCN 9798571056281

"...I don't know if you write letters or if
(if) you panic on the phone: I'd like to call you, all the same.
...if you want to, I am game."
       -Lisa Hannigan (<u>Sea Sew</u>, 2008)

Invocation.

To the women that (and continue to) inspire us all may the inspiration you gave to each we & everyone mean something ever much more to the many of them yet

to witness/be...

> *"they come in bent-backed (creaky 'cross the floor all*
> *dressed in black)*
> *Candles, thick as pillars – you can buy one off the floor...*
> *...and the ceilings painted gold (and Mary's hair is red)*
> *...and they all come here to kiss, their dead.*
>
> *-Spirit of the West ("If Venice Is Sinking", 1993)*

toc

"Sha la, la, la, la, my lady
In the sun with your hair undone
...can you hear me now calling your name from across the bay?"
-Jay Ferguson ("Thunder Island", 1977)

"Sha la, la, la, la, my lady
In the sun with your hair undone
...can you hear me now calling your name from across the bay?"
-Jay Ferguson ("Thunder Island", 1977)

"Sha la, la, la, la, my lady
In the sun with your hair undone
...can you hear me now calling your name from across the bay?"
-Jay Ferguson ("Thunder Island", 1977)

"Sha la, la, la, la, my lady
In the sun with your hair undone
...can you hear me now calling your name from across the bay?"
-Jay Ferguson ("Thunder Island", 1977)

August Blue

Slow, slow the walk past
faces that knew us not, not
their own desires, laid bare not any
a land that is curvaceous, and loud (yet calling yell)

Their passions held, hidden beneath a booger smile I
Grow weary on a maidens name.

All of them slowly bored,
Firecrackers waiting to alight,
Fatals seeking all the gloomy corners.
Waiting, holding such dreams at night. Together

they would make mighty horde
A quake to break the mountain side
Scratching, nibbling away at our hearts,
Instead, we must be the men,
Those meant to first bend before breaking
Quiet molds who must endure,
Enough for two; enough at least,
to lessen the drama.
If the occasion is right.
Quiet solitude of the many others.

We lie to them,
We kick and beat and scratch them down,
But we also cannot help but love them,
Will not help the fleeting chase
Hold them close,
For fear the blowback,
Fear the scent in our own souls.

This, this parchment I write for them,
The women that define us, guide us, mind us all.

(May it tend them well)

Chocolate in mouth w/ mint
 It is flavor of: scandalous adventure calling.
Of warmth, sliding.

slowly.

down.
my.
throat.

Giving forked tongues & blowjobs in the softened light.
Thinking aloud that fingers should not bend so far.
Guessing that jaws cannot extend nor receive.

An entire world and a girl?

It is not spandrel glass,
nor cut threads or applause:
this is the way love is starting to feel.

Gone to Goldfish Tea

Who am I, to sojourn inside?
This kindly place, all of stone,
Here, where we had written to exchange,
Me for the first time, her to judge.
(Both ready for the gallows plunge?)

We are guarded, duelists ready
Cocked hammers prepared to fly,
Enough time to laugh behind a smile,
Tongues ready to flicker at the sign.
While expecting to see London Ivy creeping,

Slipping tendrils around loose hearts.
I stood, thereby wishing to sit afloor
Watching her first, calculated movements
The steady clack of polished nail,
high upon the card, lips lightly pursed:

…she has partaken once before,
this ordering game.
Her poison a sitting, ready smile,
and today her sign is gin.
Today .

Ahh, dearest dank apothecary shop
Whose guts contain we two,
exchanging soft touches between drinks
Providing a front to guarded minds
Long glances over dark thoughts and lauded riddles,

Slicing fingertips on the parchment, giggling
Her choice being mine, mine being spiked.
A booze, not of liquid exchanges
But not yet of love held close.
Only enough to scent her smile.

I glanced up upon the first sip,
Expecting an ankle weave or wave,
Instead finding small cuts to wary knees
Of hazel circling a dilated darkness
Following traceries of
Silk 'kerchifs ready for loose, empty throats

Her eyes, a flecked red in the darkness,
Teeth gnawed, some dulled,
At least five glowing brightly
spiked arrows: when will they call out?
Are they ready to gnaw my breast and hump?

Stifled in a handshake
Yet underscored with a grin
Oh yes, those thirty white horses
All in a line and cooing.
Ready to consume me whole.

I am a ravine, carved in dank clay
Little rivulets of blood filling,
A sweat-stain worthy of rising,
She drinks, long and heartily
Of a soul ready to give and be receiven

I am hers.
For now.
Follow us now, down.
Into the mud of my mind.
We lie.

Little Red Dust

The letters now, collect upon the shelf
Gather upon naped box filling, wetness spilling out,
down the hall, far along the rug
(at least as far as the near doorstep)

A mountain grown upon the stoop
Envelopes caught in all near trees,
The passerbys, each kicking trails along,
The little dust that comes upon the ripping,
The tearing sounds which make us sneeze.
Of grinding pulp out into damp pavement
(The river is full of my words,)
Ink drawn down.
Die now.
(Drown)

I went out to buy a pen,
Let the ships carry ink from Indies east,
Far west to where the sun rises on my life,

A foul thing, a cardboard ring
Held in far too many boxes.
What is it, to fall for the taken girl?
To watch her soft embraces on strange skin
or fantasize quickly, with a steady hand?
When these things come, the come quickly

The discharge dries upon the fabric,
Seeping into the air caught between spaces,
Gathering upon a molecule to invade near nostrils,
A rotted scent, which at first sup
Makes tongue seek lips, or dried teeth space

Did you read the messages held, or burn the sound away,
Of my words, head held and expensive taste,

The postage was expensive,
The forms well wrote, triple crossed, I dotted
The items contained meant for the soul.
I love you, loved you, always will.
The hands begin to wrinkle.
The dogs die in the pits.
Outside my window a car passes.

Oh You..

Your job, sweet willingness, was to keep her still
To do it all, to be the love that never fades,
To watch the players dunk on hoops,
Consonants in a broken tongue.
Never fails to step it up, go to all the little games
Remember the names of all the people,
All the names I got the joy to forget,
I see you lived up to none of this,
Should you burst asunder,
Let a maker punish upon the sign?
Dear you, adieu to You who haunt my dreams.

My Bozeman Girl

"Held sir, fast sir! This body is shaking; its bleeding doth away."

It took ten hours - yes *ten hours* & a decade just to be (here's me)
sliding over back roads, sighing as I scour asphalt, sing hymns;
traveling east again for a heart, my soul, maybe mountaintops or
the bit of a girl I knew is left to hold & wondering if God ordains.

Six odd years of trouble I've seen converting this Virginia mind tow
ard supper, no lover -gave bug hugs, tried 2be everything as we all
caught on a cord of promise & restraint. Died w/ warriors at dawn.
I done cried, sighed beside long nights - drew battle lines deep.

Just to get this girl to turn, to earn a flutter and a chance, Bozeman
girl, pretty world – all great things to those that wait indeed except,
well where my heart burns broken, my mind gone crooked, wailing,
moving on to such ineptitude left unspoken. Being the, seeing the..

So cry on, sweet princess of delight, drive a mind to break to take.
Be everything that time & hope & love & we were meant to be. See
all the ways a life was meant to drive steaks through such doth
vampires scuttling across wide fields; poppies below hilltops.

Oh Bozeman girl, you'll leave me trapped within this strange make
believe world – one where we can rise and win, frolic & spin, best
hurt along joy & passion somehow coexist in a single frame – that
shame is what books we wrote to burn them, Bozeman world, hurt

girl how you cut me, dare me to feel like this; oh loving girl I do not
know I do not bow to that world, least I trip again, fall down along
on strange wine, subtle times. Oh, least I stumble again, into you,
into me - into now something real?

So catch me, wretch me, let me die on wonton fictitious four lane
tumbleweed bothers over wide empties where martyrs lie; hold on
as a woman can do in a certain time, a common rhythm, a
wretched catching wonton man made to be.

Lean lady learn; turn yourself to find some Son,
Take baby, need - have yourself some fun for a change. Thus,

satisfied satisfactorily untied w/ a steel line in nostrils flare fading.
Back to the land, back to the bracken molds sand up buttcracks.
Then drive on, cry on, strive there as you love them more. Love,
you'll still be our girl. You'll still be that word I spoke upon, a date I

simply never knew.

Feeling Travertine

..this place, it screams of Halloween
An entire dusty landscape, waiting just for a pry,
The lids to delve so deep: what then, where how
Whatever of a soul to take?

Like others I pined for cheap costumed thrills
A kiss upon the midnight streetside theatre grew
Or else such strange sights to fill me with temptation! Fighting
the slipping, forgetful lore, of all the sliding passages

That tear upon the human heart, or
need this inner cry, of thirstless wanton desire, yes:

I found it in such a place once, not
Knowing that I was then so utterly, truly alive.
The main drag full of whistling cold, the bleak
Of a crooked lampshade beside that sidewalk glows
Up high, so high as to call me onward.

Its light did not show me many human things, I
basking in such endless future, that was even then
Like the sun, the moon around waning, wasting
I did not know, babe, I simply did not know, but
We smiled as we danced round that flame,
did we not?

We made the most, and like the withering glow
Did hold each other so utterly, terribly close.
Crying, daring the dark to threaten how it could
Gave each other a spark, by which to set next year alight

A hope, dug too deep for fallow snow.

So let the eyes feast on this colored spectacle,
As the breeze stills.
As my pen slows, letting mind and heart pause so
As the day fades, as your name changed:
An important point worth remembering, worthy of saying
Adieu.

Miles Missing 1

Six months (seven more than necessary) to visit here! To find her
out (that da same songs in different town brings tears), no relief, so
come down and cut and scream and claim me! (-no not that side-)
high dont you see whats really there; clouds swirl round (happens);
of times & things and missionary tabularlaries yet to be? There

is silence out here on a hardscape I knew not, open wounds call
(some would say it ho-de-I, not I-da-fall) en least trees grow wide, I
supped in that resistance there, a love certainly not left now lost:
time I simply wont regain, can't recover, meet, be. (The same?)

You feared the loud, a call, the simple swelling of my lungs! The
yelling such screaming nor the simple way that I desire, need
in swelling tugs will make my soft blood rivulets run heliograms;
guts that wrench wide, hate that cackles (dis is not who I want to)

be it the sound that hollers in a way I could not anticipate, the hills
they distort the calls! They give reason to folds the night, heights
of the crowd below falls in frothing fermented formats, their gums,
such listless teeth they try to pull long, only yank out (a spell?) the

old native mounds are rising girl: dirt will soon keel over, oh you
oh girl oh person that I wanted to hold then with a chance - what
stories, what rounded stones do we know? For you knew not of
eastern toils or Atlantic madness nor the means 2 ending doom. 4

to stab oneself in the neck, it is divine, the throb of life fading beat;
a chest, or to pull out one's veins so slowly, new threads paint
glass chapels for those who are only paid to dust, the
past idiots feeding quick to rise. *For you knew not, could not tell.

(Sure you supposed these in your own way, we all do), but the
sights we carry on, from one churchyard to the other, such matters
in its the scent of old dust in attic unseen, it's the bassinet
cradling poets mind rotting beside the crème, it's the

time of day (a day late) & a storied shame, it's a, the very night a
stuck there thus alone, the hollers in the home, the way we say our

very things you know so well & probably should not but speak of. I
quake & once more an orb flies freely upon the day (your name)
the clouds around, found that these same songs in different towns
swelling of promises make my soft blood run cold this

cryptographic cover: these rotten times they call now out. (Slow).

Miles Missing (Too)

Its different, each every day & in those simple wanderings we seek someone else to trust (children thus a lust crestfallen) then to list, a hard song came on and I am broken, shifted once yet thus to be screaming into ochre air (the cherubs settle over) & flying high I

Miss miles flying by - why did your strong arms wrap around? Why did you do your best to serve & starve & attempt to obey, but not to claim or shame or maim the very fiber of my bones & though while I listen to you now oh so very deeply wide call I, while I cried & I

called! & attempted not to b me (why would you let me be that silly)

Why would u not let it/me be me? (Why not see the me yet to be?) Sure, it's the American way – that real rot that forms foundations in glass castles we know not, grow tall & let wind rattle through bones (in dreaming u found a fool who loves). Not u a moment of waking

he who needs & behaves as be, can see (with thee) be oh ME!

From above we must seem as one pinpoint spiraling, a contagion massing madness connecting settling again, ear to ear on, each other doing what we can-sliding as filaments amongst the others, one mass of hair slipping by oh runs and cuts to smash his own

face into the very boards of trees (my knees), the weeds, the grass around we fails, grows taller; he knows better & in the end somehow does the right thing amongst blossoms, dead grown tall he wallows, hates upon a breast (remembers all the rest), a WIFE!

is a person to be trusted with a life. He is I thus I'm, trusts you, you & yours (& would give that which means so much away) the cane blades cut through air immemorial. I remain immortal w/ only a flicking of a pen (my dear fem speak, amen!) & a man will swoop

down & slices now, short frames he doesn't know the what or else to do, but can learn he doesn't know what to wear, but can only observe he seems to be having a hard time, but wont rhythm, dont wont we all wish good things: neighbor coming nearer? I cry, I

wanted to love you, to admire the way your belly grows, the way your form would feel pressed against softer parts of me of mine the way each day suddenly glows Bright! I sought nothing more, not happening now, celestial choice it seems, not of my bearing then...

Not o this earth, something of rot, of clay (earth): may it have been enough.

Gnome'd

These days they feel the same; I look back now on how I slid upon
the strange times-the many flowers laid side by side, end2end & all
(diatribes & fetters they are worthy now to share) the letters seem
endlessly collect upon shelf; heed them hard, take them well!!

Day 1.

I slipped today, fell upon my nose, cursing all the foolish luck as
an attempt to rise yet splayed there stick stuck, floundered upon
the kitchen floor; astonished at the sight thus grown beside! beheld
there on supple linoleum tiles below, a shifting, a glowing (a sign)..

for 4 lines had formed, each drawn outwards from the middle, they
connected at the right angles, arrayed funny like; a hole! There a
small window to a room filled with morning rays, pristine orb gaily
shown out clearly where no such thing should at once be held! I..

Gape I did for too long, as within that portal lay a view of a bed,
posters, and (my god!) a girl resting there softly upon the spread!
Crafting dainty movements as she wiggled, my eyes adjusted in
disbelief as such moments reached out to claim me (shame me) I

"surely I must have hit my head", thought I, noticing blood drippage
collecting at the edges, dropping in only 2 fill the cracks, bright light
spreading outwards to illuminate that; a form. Yet she remained a
reigning queen of yogi fluidness, of linen on cut knee each curve

demanding a need 4 supple touch. Alas, tested weight held, sharp
objects could not pierce through, so sputter & jump did I along
this window of impossible strength (it held)! My will did not, &
…and slowly, most certainly, surely, I realized that I did not dream.

Day 2.

The nearest neighbors came when called hither, but they did not,
could not see that lass, nor imagine; I, all alone to witness this girl,
(thankfully not committed for such thoughts), only clumsily gripped,
churning continuously with worried furor at what to do! The floor...

I thought restful slumber each eve would ease troubled mind, that
Hard drink or mild drugs near & neat effects able to calm a growing
Calamity missed there by bare inches, yet, first peek at crack of
day did display something easier than expects, nothing changed, I,

She still there, a view down to a girl dreaming (scheming).
Still a gleam now grows within the kitchen, the woman still a sitting
So bored she lies around, flipping end to end (as my mind does)

Dropped my coffee mug here amongst the leaves it shattered
(Placed my hand upon the sheen, it matters! Still? Something?)

my cat does not like these wears, her fur poofballs gather tumbled
waters merely drying 'round, my hollers echo off the walls, she
dances round the brighter part of my kitchen crying, hurts head to.
(my digits wish to do right!) how do I explain there is another sight?

...it is a slow glow grown in fallen evening & I (or at least the better)
parts of all this grey day (matter) seem to have become entranced.

Day 5.

She's a soap bubble I see when turning 'round, studied best when
nibbling upon thin breakfasts, her there smiling lightly as I near just
writing a tome I cannot see! Perhaps a journal or a log of longing,
of lonely days (what words I can only guess upon), how it takes, its

Madness, surely, yet every glance eases tired mind, forgetting
much of past lives (other times), sheets (anything really)
over this 'portal' have not stayed long I confess; I gandered, I
staired longingly at this nymph, at this sullen sight 2soon 2 wander.

Friends! now wondering at my change, excuses all gather on the
doorstep, my counters overflow with detritus, takeout boxes, all I
creep there as a watched thief in the night, all corners & my own
eyes are watching now, For this light is life, livening up unlit days.

this causes need 4 instant abatement (shame then; was feeling ok)

Day 11.

She dances today, she babbles but I cannot hear (the words)
seeking closure within a blink. I cannot tarry away long, cant *think*
no do not Weekend residence here with strong brews, keep movin
to discover the rituals, movements; shifts along blurred lines I hide.

For the sun sets quick now, lite dusting of snows threatens close
but a bright gleam dances upon her brow, a small smiles forms
one which has contagioned my day with beauty, made each
MoLD! Evening a radiant sheen by which to hold – SO BOLD!

but today there were none. 2 days then without the eating; I fear, I
worry she is either a delusion or elf, taking they that yes I am
stuck w/ in her beautiful cage, but happy! *(I am? Am I?)* this
Dearest Puck which has infected my day, take this (take this)

today was just with glad tidings, so often loft yet not fear that
that the edges loosen on something more than lids, I grow, I.

(Hold me tome, let these supple eyes do more than see...)

What does this mean? The floor gives slightly, such corners lift,
mere inches now smear into the bright of son catching close, I
rose! lancing upon dear braced agony, I fell, I
down upon my tiled galley, a drop of (sweat?) seek not to try hard I

no pictures cannot capture, no lofty things but I
it is her!, looking up just brushing her waving hair. Her..

Oblivious to the

I tripped on the damn thing on entering, in such efforts, she looks
up to ignore or perhaps pretend: the other choice is there, yes, a
a normal life ignored, stubbed just as my toes are (got2 go away)
My sigth is gone, my tastes bubs superb, my lady a (she sits there)

waiting creature caught now in a day, this room. (She calls?)

Woke from a light snooze, and found myself TRAPPED! Where?

Wander everywhere but follow a simple path
home to the yellow browns that form the boarders,
still convinced I still see this girl, living!
…there is something now there, lying ahead.

Day: *Unknown?!?!*

Like any spy, I have in fallen too deeply, given in
IN to my respite, desires consuming dearly, sup sweet vam
pire to given up on rest, or food, the subtle, meandering HATE I
I am like she, a prisoner there forever staring outwards, ripped

Up all *the floorboards* all the passing's of a troubled mind what is?
Work can go threw the halfway point, where did the sun go? I

Tortured is of our love (for now), I can see, I
I can read her notes now – like my heart she calls, she holds up a
calling neither bathing, nor growing she paints shaped toes, sitting
there Ever waiting, bating me on she. (Her eyes they suck me in!)

I rest here. I gaze about there. Anywhere but here, there, I, any
where And from time to time I gaze over my shoulder, I watch, I
see To ensure there is not a another watcher there is
not watching thus a me. watch. What. *All We Do Is Watch!*

I think I now will pray, an attempt to at least thus lean inside. I
(or else learn to rip up upon the boards, the shoring, the fl..the...fl..)
Fin.
There is now a creaking sound, a loud, a crackling... I..

A Note from Neighbor Adam:
I went o'er to Jacob's house this morning,
worried how he has missed two weeks' worth of time of us, of
card games, hellos, simple ceremonies all religiously attended
before this business of a joke, a "window" upon his kitchen floor.

4 heart attacks (&suicides) do happen, life can thus fade away, but
it seems neither held sway considering what I saw upon approach;
eerily the back door was left ajar as were all lights were on, the
simple calls went unanswered, the whole house utterly silent walls.

This entire place now devoid of furniture, of
inhabitants, with only one object of note: that of
A framed picture left in that location; of he...

...and the woman once described...
(both smiling)

The above tome left upon the counter side make me worry, & even
The picture seems heavier than I'd like to hold, I think
I'll leave it to sit here a while, let authorities curse & worry now

This time forever evermore.

-End Rambles-

`Curl Sleep

That boy is drowning, we did not know; water constriction
working successfully, clogging up capillaries fast, membranes
giving way to saline solution pickling thin, turn into themselves, he
heard a rumor there, a nugget in a tale & now he has to...wander.

For these things can no longer considered funny, nor should they
thusly be ignored; a deluge worth of insults battering, spiraling,
outward, falling quick, torn asunder after, all...
...but one still best when told from the beginning.

So:

Jokerman, grinning man, he entered quick here w/ a smile, buried
three rounds in Carolyn's scalp, one each in temple, hairline, then
upper nub respectably yesterday eve - a dog ear's night as the
fireflies sailed, the gypsies wailed, & all danced round so haughtily.

It was the close-kiss-love type w/ a sneer, a reprisal within a song;
left then thus accordingly, happy with his tale, delighted further still
that his point was made, the grave would feed, all love & the town
'sfolk soon would cry.

In time a boy came then there simply to close those riveted eyes,
seal the smoking holes which catch all slipping tears
the damp carbon that hardens upon a cheek side.
It fractured even upon generous face below, that which is

still determined so not to weep.
He cut hard by the sight, so deeply that he must have collapsed,
but woken shortly by the smell, the purification thus arising.
Hating the day, hating his life, hurtfully knowing that he

aint gunna be saving a princess anytime tonight.

Carried my....his love in an old cart down to the wishing well, the
tone that carries to the sea, the one that cleanses so.
Stiffened not still illustrious to feel, her one foot ready for glass a
good slipper then to tune while humming.

Beautiful hair story, a lament song;
float on instead in the jetsam when dropped.
Give young boys as myself, a Bleu-green look of
continued love, a hated stair while passing,.

So wave not dear Carolyn, your
imagined fingers will curl slowly, bloat there in the cold, fire
of icy bottom mud; toes dip-drag in minuette position.
Giving you a reason now to dance, dear prisoner of the current.

(Besides, you wont wait long; this boy is also drowning.)

If I were strong, a taunt muscle flex and not delicate
I could cry, not near the village as a broken soul.
Reel past the colors coming off the tepid river front,
celluloid glow giving the insides a name; not red, not dark...

(...lord, anything but a crimson feel.)

Shapes, shades, all reflections catch on silverware held.
The windows too, silent while passing, houses are close beside,
as the pathway begins to blacken, slowly brains thus drift away,
God even weeping silently, weightlessly – a shade beside the day.

I...he sees her in the moonbeams, a bobber fast to snap.
She taps time silently in the ocean waves, somewhere dearly
to settle along further on, curl-sleep, falling deep:
encouraging the version of how a man should look. And act.

While beckoning for another one to join her.

So dear nicotine laced enhancement, the parchment for the pen,
His time to sleep is coming, a distance nearing held.
I fell there, near there; but still in love with that smile.

Take my hand then as I near, help me sleep then for
A little while.

Adieu.

Other Name

She's the only one whose potent
Ink on my page is caught, drawn in
Tones of teal on bars of silk not
Pausing nearby respiration or else
Taking time to break our nostrils open.

She is my sweet automation,
Encyclopedia of misconduct open
To misconstrued answers, guts, and so many bugs!
Curved from knees to feet, hand to bleed
Sweetness in of my lips to part, not sharp, not

All the things I need or yet still wish to be.
A ships steel sunk to need – sleek, and deathly proud,
Curl her toes to the point tip, a rune to rub, a
Vein to poke or capture, or with such love to and
Then dance these nights away.

Forgive me, I peeked at the sight
Bare bottom exposed then to summer sun.
You don't notice your care, you curse, your cars are
Filthy now, broken glass in chocolate melt
taking time swerving on busy streets.

This kindly place, all of stone,
Here, where we had written to exchange,
And then I to die in (of?) ecstasy, or perhaps
For another moment, another love,
Another name by which to fail its all only just the same.

A timid pattern yet to break.

Sea Song

The North Sea means something different
to the Celtic folk clinging 'long its shore
Sea spell causing their voices to ring haughtily.

Those that wish to sing, those that remember how.
To each, that endless drowning desert
holds a spell beyond the life

They come forth to remember, pay tribute;
for the dead sometimes come in with the tide,
shapeless forms lying just beyond the wave break.

Foam has a purpose of description
One foot, then next, trying not to stumble
these living crowds that edge the cliff side.

Do not wish to join the legion below.
In goes sandalwood, monkshood

Thin Celtic girl of my dreaming evening ends
I am just born a metal workers son
Stamped out of pride & smells, no salt

Standing upon this listless shore
alone, listening to the waves crashing in.
Not Roman Catholic, and that way I'll stay.

Clap upon the surface, where to burn & splinter; writhing
in an attempt to remove a scratch

The Function of a Woman

Wit, of course, alongside fortunes folly growing, the very hilarious
simple notion that this is love (she, her ways) I along w/ all men
can get caught in that trap; straps twist sideways on open arms,
wrists grace my chin pull hard; ears became held thus as destiny a

heart captured soon upon the swoon of a clotted mind, rotted I
did not wander Manchurian courtyards, not Montezuma halls, I
gaze only upon fine moon growing, bosom now a showing (O dear
supple rays thus hold me, take me close): allow me deep to sup oh

Martha, if I could tell you enough to fill your wagging gourd, a
laugh beside as tectonic shifts would fill the wound, long plains to a
a grave yes thus to take me; awake 2 spill the guts beside (cruelly)
at the thinking that maybe this is all, it could be worse, grab broom.

Swat whatever winds will sew, blow out da better part o me, but as
gravity took hold (a falling down to madness) mattress I beheld
another tale growing wide, spinning round, slick fingers reach up to
claim daintiness, no – not when they hold the knife, not when (not)

glances fill up phones; a clattering of hands & long gossip, the
flecks they are gathering soon, then, in ruinous second guesses
everything begins to settle (my mind feels so brittle) – it gives! It is

the foundation of a woman too, that important thing, a soul swoon
singing up through tumbled weeds in grass grow by the wayside,
roadside mud (do not fall there), serrated hooks & meat (not me)
struggling to remember the writer of cheap books, looks piled high.

That way she dances funnily on the beach before the breaking:
I never knew that side (only racism before breakfast) a nook a
tongue so full of sand, scrapping along the way, my backside.

The future of a woman is, everything I wish I need it to be, not
spent grain in open graves, not earthworm's paradise to roam, not
I nor loam or a mobile full of memories now, memes pulling me

back to myself; I cast runes by the candles light of screens I see
lies & lines growing, I witness cognitive divide (like to watch, a
jump &pretend: 2hide?) – peace now, slow as a surprised soft pen:
a daggerside slides inside her (I know that soon I'll be a going).

*(Falling there, if only on a feeling)

Please all I ask is that you thus take my hand.
(Trust in it, in me) if only for a (*Little while).

Fall then on a feeling: I promise soon to put the blades thus away.

Please all I ask is that you thus, to take (my hand).

Woa, man

The primal forests were never as dark,
More delightfully twisted than any the maps man made seem
Twisted now; seem to fall somewhere within.

For the terrifying creatures that dwell here, there
Are automatons, not born of flesh and bone, they
scale the walls, they merely drill through masonry and stone
Somehow ignore the windows of my soul, my meal, the meat;
Jump through windows, to access newborn children swollen.

Cuz this morning, a devil awoke me, cared -
Remains of pure glass in soft wood contained, solid guts;
Brick held, and mortar too – both to remined me of reality crumbled
The gravity of the situation, pulling at us, yanking such everything
Apart.

Black window on high; why not enter in?
It is not the maelstrom's fury, or the hard tongue grasping fast
Of a woman, left to want, to need, to rot
Or the hard tongue of a girl left to not, no, there is…he. That,
Of a who, a man; I climb, upon visages above hallowed rooftops
I, hating the exercise, despising the feel of soot on hand & fingertip

Above the grey dawn wishing and needing and wanting to dispel ;
Catching neither melancholy, or myself unawares.

Up then, towards that, an opening, glazing all around, I (oh I)…

Oh dark slit, in he who tarries in the face of red, fallow worry.
How I want a silken, craven thing that comes breaking from within.
Like your own folly, equally a dark tunnel, that
one quick peek as a hope to dispel the I shattered there, startled.
My lips found your edges &
All those darkened worries waned. The worms dined deep. So

I rise, and raise again as a hope by which to thus dispel
My fingers caress your mantel, then I slip fast, irony calling,
cobbled loafers now a dangling deep,
Ready for the flying, calling for the falling, sliding, flying quicker
true, consumed
High above those sooty rooftops, born to engorge on salt, slate
Uplifting holes down there, agape
Maws then ready for the churning.

"Let foothold HOLD", my splintered mind thus cries
Wishing now, not for gold or jewels, love or fools
(Or even a revolver by which to do fell deeds)
Think, not fail fast
But instead, caught up on the thought of broken glass.

A Letter to Kate

Dear you, dearest your dreaming darkly
She who haunts my dreams.
A slow footstep on back porches crossed,
The reed sound of traipsing marshes held
The sawgrass clutches and cuts,
Greens like plastic pens
Come at me like vibrato,
Kicking legs up, turned ears to hear.

Woke up in a haze today,
A false pretense of warm
A City Beautiful,
A Detroit for Limitless Ages,
A Cleveland whose form will fall, sucking
deep on softest lips,
The sex of irrelevance.
What visions are seen when you sleep at night,
Or before twilight finds your eyes?
Before sleep catches on light shore brambles,
Gets tossed in the crags between the starfish,
Sea moss resting hopefully for spooning.

The byway plays,
I see a patience brooding,
Taking shape through art or flair,
A soft foot in this sheathing, a soft foot in simple sheathings,

A girl made of legs, not grace nor tall
Sharp muscle ready to strangle, tis all

Dear Kate,
I am structured now
Something to be stumbled upon, not
A common item; a river then of note,
Liquid only for the drowning,
Unfit for sailing ships or lovers baptisms.

Do not let me become an asterisk to your lifesong,
A footer not worth ink or scribe letter.

Where in your dreams do you go?
Out to the endless marshes,
Perhaps to the little rowboat,
Where we promised to make love.

She

Of teenage body, feel (fell)
Finding my way in, through long nights
And lots of heart beatings
Thunderous,
You always wore those crummy sweaters,

This year, I had to burn.
Fry to best learn the meaning,
Of hurt. Of sexy choices made in the fall.
All the crappy wood the mobile was made of,
Home of scrap; don't hold back.
Stuck loving this town,
You somewhere, most of all…

Hey Other Love.

It feels so wrong to put these words here,
you beside the she,
he so nearest the me, but
here it goes, anyhow...

Hey other love, I
finally got down to those other long shores, the
ones you waded upon long ago, floated there
followed them in time like you knew I always would,
called out to the open ocean with a song and a prayer
and a hope that all this would make sense somehow; could matter.

That the ink can't fall from the page, drain down the short table to
stain my shirt as it wound its way to way to the wooden floor.
Dribble off as I got lost in these tall mists, dreaming again -
that the shore wouldn't go on and on or that in my clumsiness I
would fall or jump right in, same as then, same as always.

That shattered hearts really cant do much more than break
and break and break and break,
or fall in beside the rushing waves that call to claim them.

Though your dead now in oh so many awful, so terrible of ways
though your lip is a sneer along with a mind that makes a
snarl at all the thoughts spinning round from the broken days
alongside the though of him, of me, of my voice shaking, I still
wish to say these things still mattered. I hear (heard?) you -
the days they didn't drift off outwards totally into oblivion.

You're a flash reel on the one film being screened in town, sure
(nothing to borrow, every inch to hold, listen, to follow somehow)
...but the land here is beautiful in a way that your soft feet know,
once felt here, may (hopefully) do so again, as on my heart
carved out a space, then echoed out to a place where any who
looked or tried or even dared could find them.

No more adieus you fool - not from this simple man, or any others
Its not, shouldn't ever be though of as any form of....of...of...
Fuck your weakness, fuck your entitled sense of harassment, you'll
grow one day to see that other love takes on many forms...

Good luck.

Warning.

Father earth, mother sky,
Hear my heartsong and reply!
This is where the memory starts,
Not a soapshine to recall,
Not a sheen on glowing marble,
Light fleck in the eye,
Not enough to turn astray.

Beware, beware the sight of work.

Misplaced Colors

Another red plug
here, waiting patiently
on this crisp porcelain.
Not mocking, merely resting
spooning the dust motes
and any simple bathroom grime.

It never traveled far,
sought out Ganges dreams,
or odd glances
at the back of dank bars.
Waste dump views;
the best it can hope now.

It could have waited here,
knitting strange tomes
watching shapes pass, tall
heads stuck far above nimbus,
with eons passing easily
or another hour gone by.

But still it found me
quickly without camouflage,
helped entice me to burn
merely with its shape.
A Cheshire smile;
I recognized its tale.

Immediately hated short nights
of quiet trepidation,
bathing deeply within
gentle joys of discovery.
But hating more
all the shifting walls

made merely by this color,
curling like small toes,
sturdy as the girl
who existed to shape it
hold it, mold it,
yank it to my floor.

Another will serve
as a reminder of more
that once we engaged in it,
and it was good.
Felt better than good,
bordering on great.

What am I to do
if...when I find another?
Char its sweet end,
or feed it to the first?
Hope that this second turns blue,
dies from its own stench.

But great is not enough,
not for the red,
red must be fed greatness
red must not be made aware
of mistakes allowable,
even if red errs itself.

But I am an artist,
and this color
remains as one -
many is my palate
by which to craft,
to create something bolder.

We are meant to avoid
mixture of such dense flavors,
because orange is stronger still,
something once possible from we two;
it is trauma overcome,
and thus could never be.

Poet's Dance

watch the little swallow, delicate
hobble from toe to toe in the cold
oh, the illusion! that i could fall for such a pretty thing
just rub a finger against her breast

such delusions of my mind
only mean that i have gotten caught up in the movement
the tight constriction that comes from an angry, vocal taunt
much as in her heart

this evil nymph, i'm afraid she has come to steal my soul
seeking the color of a flushed cheek
a color i'm sure that will trail after her when she flies
startled now, such a jittery thing

Nobody Bowing

It's a strange sight to break the Masters hold, a notebook there
in hand to hold the fading sighs & stars all turning crisply to white.

The sky is only lightly tinged now, cool there, cloudy.
The sun still shines through in patches, sometimes I,
Expecting to see a hand break through the nimbus crying, a
Choke up my cheek so tell me then to slow;
Turn baby, turn by which to burn.

The vessel prepared its own rouse,
Space invader on the move; its on yeah. So
I'm a corn popper coming for you! You drive
Me wild so crazy sure, *certain* you
infect my brains, for that I
bleed away, for love.

Just you keep your electric eye on me, ignore the
burning of the world, the turning of the girl, the
Passing of the simple torchlight in your hair,
Watch my eyes, dear grown up doll, you falling fast
I see those pupils dilate, can
That hazel rimmed dark swallow a soul?
Red hair too, edges of the tips
Dyed as such, dying
more.

So scrape me off the surface of the world, brick;
It's that thing that fills you and empties everything else,
All at once, watching your soul dribble out through your toes
Don't let it go. (Boredom now, in folds – don't explode).
For today she asked me what it is
To cheat.

Showers Cold & Simple

This eve is a movie frame, and I
am bathed in electric light.
Audiences bored at the trying drama,
but this is my life: fast forward.

I wander at night.
Do not know where I go.
Thoroughfares transversed.
Hint of canopies under shade with midway shine;
August boughs leaning down to run

twiggy fingers through my locks.
These eyes are now unwilling or unable to rest
mostly consist of pupils, seen not, but seen enough
not reflections caught   ----   glimpsed, revered. Held.

Oh, God, can you hear me?
Can I even hear myself?

Shatter

The Day after shatter, stuck between the rail and concrete, dry
day with a squint in eye, we descended downwards along new tile,
fall up along hard streets: stairs of (un)even cut in long drop, there.

(Sielth coming nearer)

The Day after laughter, sharpest gunshot to my face I bathed
in the shadows of your palm fronds, somehow grown in this land,
disguised myself in sweat in order to see, a need; a seed pod be
something that minutely folds, clever holds - da gate opens widely.

With my own eyes the extent of such deceit becomes clearer, for
I am awaiting for your artistic moment, stuck beside dogs walking
the same pond each afternoon, leash held as modern noose, a
calling to the night, everything alight & somehow then screaming.

This is me patiently waiting, falling into cliché, stuck deep in debris,
Shot for the stars but floundered on Mars I am a hotshot yearning
Only to burned in the stick sweet of the atmosphere, not on entry
but on the slicing up of skin where parting seas reflects poorly me.

I have drunk those white drops, sipped upon
A hot elixir for heavy tongues, collapsed fast near
Wet grass where all bodies go for the rotting, I
Uncertain amongst the morgue – decay comes there too.

Scared now to reenter (if I barely survived the climb) the tomb
Spinning somewhere here surrounded by light, cutting deep.
Supposed to feel right. Talking to the bright, madness now, I
Loved her enough then to think about, considering now, to

Leave her.

Royal Woods

A Women. That Woman.
The Woman,

She managed to earn a place under my skin,
Not sure with fine precision or just weakness of mind;
A fatal there to stay, to root around like so many gerbils nesting.
Held precious, but mentally removed with much disdain.

Held, I say, because I asked her to enter and stay,
made room amongst all the decent clutter.
Precious, I say, because I realized far too late
what little caught was more than friendship.

I..

I dreamed of my City darkly, no windows;
Everywhere an endless sea of wood beams.
Shades smirking over cups of tea.
Always watching; faint glows from reflected pupils.

I meandered here along a Seine that never existed,
Dreading the waking, the screaming that follows.
Saw her hair at a distance, riding that broken bicycle,
Red, and always seeming to ride away – always laughing so

Follow me out, past the edge of the quai's,
To where our favorite colors collide – hallucinogen times;
Those crafting a scene I will remember when down,
Drawn up and drugged against a better state of mind.

The Alligator and the Gun

There's a girl down along the shore a crying,
In Lido, amongst all the laced keys
Where sunshine burns sky away,
Another he-haw girl; another nightly name.

Oh lord, send me a crisp wind to play,
Burn this soul in seas of orange,
Drown me in a hurricane
Take this note on up to the Mackinaw Bend
This story, all the way too the end

There's a lady, on the balcony dancing 'way
Timing wither her infant, beat by tired feet
Swing that face to the time of the sand shift,
Shore dunes swaggering way on a
Swing
Say, say goodbye to the end of the day
Greeting the lights rising off the surf,
A twinkle caught on the ocean teal of time
Witch tunes that glow in the streets
Through all the sawgrass, where we lost blood

Passenger

Burn, dear nicotine laced
Enhancement of another name; a sight of better days;

let me watch your embers fall.
Colored things that no longer hold sway
- you are a reminder of late nights, of dear troubles held.

enhancement,
just dissolve away

Let me breathe such sighs to the night air,
To release; to die somewhere
 in endless longing.
Listen to me speak, and be forth wise.
This is the tale to tell:

A clouded eve that was strange to behold,
Blurry edges that defined a kept vision,
Passenger to my own life, drifting towards the obvious,
Oblivious to everyone but me and strong drink.

She was wandering through the crowd,
A marked victim unawares of sharp teeth all around,
And I – a humble neighbor wishing safe passage.
Do I wear a cloak of positivity as well?
A shrouded tale of incompetence?
Do I cut and tear and scream.

She stumbled at me in the darkness,
I, codgering the many mental tricks to get her home,
Her, not realizing yet that I actually cared,
I, not yet realizing the scent of desire.

When she first ran from me, I almost determined to let her go
Leaving battered keys in the knob to twist open,
Laughing at her, her almost cartwheeling down 40 sets of stairs,
Arriving on collard bricks in some form bludgeoned.

Yet somehow in those wanderings,
I conveyed compassion sincere
Genuinely held and turned the key,
The second time she ran, I followed still
To silken sheets, many bad choices held close.

The way she held me – so determined and trusting,
I couldn't help but swoon – to let her heart attach,
This I was surprised, after the many wanderings after
And with the tucking her in to bed, she called my name

Took my hand to supple breast, turned another lock
And challenged me to love.

She was taken aback by my sincerity to care,
Likely ashamed to be discarded so easily,
So quickly as not to be worth a mans while.
She was beautiful, and did not need this man to love.
But my weak spot has always been compassion and a challenge,
And wanting to show her she was worth the beauty resolved,
A steady hand, a pounding breast
The feel as she forced the product upon myself,
Me relishing the thought, was thought all is was?

So I loved hard, I loved fast
I loved by every stroke of the pen and insertion of ink.
To raise a spirit in my mistresses circle.

When she came to me, it was with trembling hands
Ringed fingers that each thanked my nape,
Their own way scarring flesh behind open lobes,
And a simple clutching to my frame that stole seed,

My room, hidden in dreams, is not a place to tread lightly.

Day After Shatter (Not Her..)

You were free, released this time with gentle hands
Allowed, for once, to offer the help needed to change a tune

But these same church bells are now churning,
Wind this time, in fine crippling blasts,
Where once was hot and dead and buried.
Drifts slowly.
But don't you feel it? The summer whisper of trees nearing?
We will hear it for you, sifting down
We are at war with ourselves,
In ships with painted sails.
Why would you paint the sails?

The dreadful machine, it must start once again
Needing living cogs by which to run, turn it's gears on mortal flesh
The kind that want to run,
The omen in the darkness,
Not this – anything else but the shattered lives,
The hardening of fists and the miscommunication of desire.

In such gasps of life, we found a second beauty, another hate
Another hate
So many Laertes similar, an echo to deceive

But the wind through the bark, it eases
The river stays its own course for a change
If for a little while more, down,
out, flung somewhere into the sea
Far beyond, where all things go in time

This, a haunted place, but still so beautiful.
omen. That Woman. The way she watches her hands,
Opening, folding, hoping for someplace to rest.
Rest now, for morning comes.

*"...don't wanna touch you but you're under my skin
(I wanna taste you too) but your lips are such ven-o-mous"*
-Alice Cooper ("Poison", 1989)

Trigger Happy

This Canadian girl feigns love
                whenever I visit her evening bedside.
Sheets. Tangles. We've discovered the meaning of boredom.

This nymph, she wreaths
smoldering curls which tumble along fair nape;
 to suckle tempered nipples cupped between knuckle cusps.

A minuet of noses, then apologies tongued,
because sexless we've lain &
I did not let this small girl (or my heart) deceive me.

We surround ourselves with toys from her innocence
as she beckons me to place one in her asshole;
desiring to get off on a different sort of feel.

It was enough just to hold her.
To need her still.

Every tenth frame we are allowed to sample each other,
pin one other viciously before mind wakes from gutter,
foretasting this English morn as it bleeds skyward;
an October clarity.

Stirring parents & alarm clock hum remind me that time is short;
that penetrations are temporal.

Meanwhile I'll persist on the simple knowledge
that she wants to fuck me
...and I wont let her.

The Prudent Doctor

Beneath the scent, and the smell of smells
The gross disgust that issues from slime coating
Of hands growing?
Of hands plunged deep in soft afterbirth
A form that comes before the wriggling form.

This is she, a patient form
She closes an eye, and it is done,
This royal boy, reaching forth to seize his world.

His hand, for a moment finds hers and recoils,
Unknown in his soft bath, all the contracting force
Of muscles upon his face, his hands again
Reach forth with little fingers that marveled at their reach
To form around forms, the little digits at last found

She retires home, a solitary place, and prays to Vishnu
Eyes below the six hands, pondering for a moment
Checking the other two

-That red/purple/green combo:
Did I imagine it?-

Time had a purpose for once this evening
and beautiful, making slow perfect sense.
Gave me courage to talk to the near moon
and every fractal pattern on the grass, each
flower stem held, and short petal torn
existed to remind me of her face.

The clock hands thrice stretched longer, green vessels
pumping through the veins: each revealed as strands
growing from her own heart's core, of course.
Its a sign of death, beauty shortly held:
of oldening slowly. But god, how
can I describe her? Her laying upon
a wavering sea of chartreuse, not seeing
not believing, but trusting me too
with all her soul to, guide us through the haze.

Both slithering, aging, growing restless with
the movement of the light: the best part.
Of my life & that entire night was
feeding her cantaloupe & being close.
Becoming shapes in the dark, twig people
who feast on such darkness as well as life,
and with the Son are reborn yet again.

In my own widening pupils I saw
death approaching fast, the end of us both
lounging; I laughed at his petty mockery.
Sat reading quotes of other safe people
to the laughing her, smiling giddily.

The trip started with soft piano tunes,
ended with I loving her. Her the same
old self she always was & will yet be.
This is a poem for she that sings life,
laughs with a smile, and plays with sink water.
That safety word has become a story,
living tattoos of the deepest clover,
coating the softest skin revealed: arms, legs.

I hope it guides her well.

Stolen from Carrie - (Barista Chicka)

There is a girl of industrial coffee make.
I long to know her outside the grind,
glimpsed at the window seat this morning,
while my cup grows warm.
Then cool; moving towards chill.

The percolator tempered fingers so keen
to curl around the edges
while she shuffles. To smile with sadness.

Place emphasis upon the sigh
as the words drip;
expressions caught,

bitterness held.
I never enjoy after that first sip.
Glare at the rinds collecting at the bottom
only meant to throw away; nestle somewhere in a waste basket.

Anne

When a man stands outside of woman,
Both must exist alongside the heightened sense,
A rouse to throw off troubled minds,
The suspicion that arise from desire.

Each sex shall turn detective to uncover,
The slight choices that come with one finger prodding
Of desire, Or endless wanderings in cities never bred.
Cut a swath through all the garbage in Chicagoland.

A long face to match long form,
Twisting sideways with bend of knee.

Or any visitors ready to fondle,

All those congested passengers waiting.
Groins maintaining condensation,
The way a hair part may signal quickness end:
There feels now masterplan, no end goal begun
Only questions with hurried answers

When a woman holds that dopey soul,
In hands she feels past kindly expectation
Does her large hat up with a pin,
Pricking her finger along the seem,

I ask: does it hurt so?
The face does not begin to wince.
I am a soft hand in the dark,
Bent fingers feeling past cleavage held,
They, drunks in the gloom,
Stumbling to cicada tunes,
Unawares at the predator's eye,
Molested in the darkness
By their fears.

An Enigma

I can imagine her, a passerby on this Canadian Shield
Endless bootsteps on plain snow,
Around an endless field, packed, all of graves

Through the ice I heard her sounds,
Past the comings and goings of many others
The wild effects of the light beseeched me
A drowning man.

Bodies content to wait, silhouetted below
She, seeing a form down below the cold,
Questioning the shapes, unsure what next to do

Deep, her fingers wet, armpits groaning
Into crusty mullions, to claim me from quiet death.
My body grew scruff just for her to grasp,
Flesh giving way instantly to touch of course fingers.

I know their feel through time; soft, small.
Face aglow with issued blue tinges,
Before I turn to her; weep at the passing.

I am not one stuck in shock
Nor immovable man, broken tale forlorn
My heart, it hums in red tones
Ours, upon meeting caught fire
A supple form to hold

Me, sitting here, not sure what next to do myself.

I watch her go with hug in hand,
Slide through the hourglass form of my door,
Love held, ass dimples showing hard,
Love, it is rippling, backward in time to warn me
Scars – they do not warn you that it will stain your lighter skin,

The Enigma is, I am allowed to fall in love
Not allowed to say it,
Allowed to share the greatest conquest,
But not to mention it by name,
To hold it and love it dearly,
But admit it only to myself
It is enough to understand humility,
Or learn, the hard way, what dreams lead to
Upon the wakening.

Every day, she comes down from the window
walking by the boy with flowers stick-stuck,
he, looking anxiously at passer-bys,
catching each in some pose or reverie.

Four times of ten she catches those soft blues
from the eye corners only, refraining.
"Ah, he is 'merican!" says she, in mind
conspiring reasons for abatement.

Has he long made up his to travel there
bouquet under arm, to view only the Seine?
A river sprite with good grin, cut features
meant to impress, and almost doing so.

Looking like those that read blog life stories,
then put his on a number; the wheel spun,
landed him on these banks, that he slowly,
soulfully may soak up the river smell.

And wait.

She giggles, thinking of writing this too;
her life, and an 'merican boy fused? PAH!
But the days never shift, and he daily
spies at her, always in recognition.

And onwards, till one dawn she awakens,

She awakens one dawn to a startling,
removed from a dream where the waters spoke,
long, slow sounds lapping at the quick edges
of her, her spectacle; nothing else more.

This time, she scents the roses wafting early,
goes to the window sill with nightgown drawn,
peering; a chance to catch sapphire rising,
with hope, wonder now in heart held.

Weast

I see the rising east, sweet history; to seek the origin of dreaming
Your eyes rest west; to that of opportunity, & the dear setting sun
West, where Mojo Rising wrote to live,
East, where he died aspiring to better days.
Both, a balance, more potent than any drug.
We, stuck in this middle and ready to run
Ready to jump and play,
To sleep and stay,
or write such simple poetry.

I. Queen of the Leaves

I sought the broken moor-fields outside London
to speak to the dead woman kneeling there
between the trunks, grin snagged in the branches.
Removed with these truanced fingers, calling,
to beseech her of a fledgling daughter:
what to do of decaying Solanaceae
amongst the shortest day of the year.

I strayed between foliage, reached skyward
with eyes so dead tired of dissolving
again & again into supple tear craft,
to deliver my amends to such myths.
Faerie: a darkness visible, to me
she spoke through dust, each minute catching word,
cotton; sharp-edge attachments on fetid breeze.

Caused a pause of breath & misstep backwards;
a falling to knees where I glimpsed her form
through the disturbance, passed cupped fingers.
While she laughed, French giggles which turned the world
word vertical, save those tortured eyes
carved upon the distance, which held dear me
crying out for simple understanding.

Shades changed as pictures turned
lounged upon the boughs till she fell cackling;
one autumn leaf dancing on spoiled air,
tempting the soil below with casual lore.
Her toes broke the earth where she touched down
clapped rigidly, then asked me to speak,
spitting violence through that beautiful smile.

I went to ask her about her daughter,
drinking heartily, blurring the edges
of my world, I asked only one word: why?
Watched the day burn off with her slow answer,
while blood fell in stages, where it striped soil
of moisture, froze into the red hardpan.
So long, the willows shifted to hemlocks.

I averted pupils for just one second,
one instant more of mute light clutching hard,
knew (heard) it was time then to leave this place.
To walk the longest road home-bound, loathing,
while I hemorrhage; one arm clasped for support.
Knowing it is time to cause a blunder.
For I'm a devil at a quick mistake;

when I make one, it takes the form of lead.

II. Les' Chemins Du Desire

When I enter a great city at dawn,
each of the hundred thousand, or million
souls contained in steel, or concrete sheathings
beckon with a sound: heartbeats subtle, true.
It's a pale comparison to deceit,
or the many rhythms that come from lies.
But enough to form the throes of pleasure.

To live in the throat of the corridor,
where she fucks hard during the dead of night.
My street starts right where the snowfall begins,
requiring marked footsteps, soft tracings
before bloodspouts can embroider such silk.
Death may often linger upon the dusk,
but has a simple soft side for high noon.

Hard drink has slowed snowsquall, but not the aim;
oddly caused pauseure before I entered
to ponder one star falling from the sky.
Is it a godhead, threading through white specks?
Perhaps an ink-spot catching the soft wick,
or the oily darkness in my blues churning?
Both startle at the disturbance of the door.

I have walked along pathways of desire,
ran sideways upon the walls as well
with a slow opening of eyes to sight
this loving girl of flame, yet not to burn.
When all choices rot, the decision seems
to murder this girl, bury her in blood;
feed her sickening stench to hungry ooze.

Dilation? I left a him new hole,
formed from all six shots of the revolver.
One to catch the softened, hallow teardrops
or finger fuck to his own heart's content.
To her, I merely took the knifes sharp point
pressed firm with a kiss, stealing the last breath
perhaps escaping forth to call my name.

Waited till the surprised eyebrows slackened,
the questioned smile slid from her naked face,
then took her form to the mud as promised.
Called out for each good citizen to hear!
Shook the golden locks in the swirling air
to show what broken promises will earn.
Walking on, clots drying on my throat, I
dropped her facedown, where none yet dare move her.

Cold Again

Cold again,
Where did the orb go?
Cold here, once again,
All is chilling bone.

What I wouldn't give for a grin.

The Constant Gardener - (to the Woman on the Grass)

When last I fell into love,
I knew all the right things
and therefore said them.

When cast out doley,
I wrote till pen & heart were dry
Nimble now, such a fractured thing beheld.

Now content to watch,
Peer into a blue that breaks from darker water,
Or cry out, to send inner beasts back into deep wilderness:

It is a composed passion, these things.

For when I first awoke into this life,
I talked like a man, fought like a god
& doing so, watched the world burn.

Upon awakening to the shambles of a new day
I relearned how to grow quiet calm,
subtly pick at the many weeds that reared their ugly heads.

I spoke, therefore I am.
I hated, therefore I am that too.
I love now, and seek a brighter future:
That has made all the difference imaginable.

My Henna Girl

Every inch of her, a dot
Speckled love, as if emerged
From under a sheet studded with fair dew.
Freckled dragon covered all in scales,
Eyelids crinkle at first opening,
First light, be it candle or flare.

One does not simply kiss this girl,
Unless seeking to stain lips and teeth,
To enter her slowly, with questioning chatter
Tongue darting in with lizard quickness,
Hold hard skull, wishing to crush
Beneath these fingertips
Lies knowledge, discontent.
I love her, every inch of her
She a bucking beast waiting to mold.
Me, a cadaver waiting for cold.

Who are you, being of the night,
Coming to me, all scents and smells forlorn,
Set your soft head upon my shoulder,
Coursing fingers through my short locks,
Unhurried, unwanted,
Speaking of love wanted, but not well known.

The middle nail is broken,
It doesn't scratch, or catch, or make a sound
But I know. I hold it close.
Watch the indigo stains beneath nails,
White. All of you is white.
It is me coming to stain,

You want to see my dark,
The dark brings out the best of light,
But it can easily match the night.
I am a fork in the gloom,
Vibrating with drunken hands,
Let me put the plug into the wall

Harbor Crossings

I asked her to speak, to me a native tongue
Stood transfixed at bent cragles,
The lines that formed around her eyes,
Transformed into shawled grand ma ma,
Insisting I finish my onion broth,
Least it grows cold upon the table.
Which softly tightens o'er her face

How could I but laugh?
Giggle at the formed delights,
Of course to offend, if but accidental!
Offend in my own language and beyond,

Can I blame non-existent night terrors,
The little tracery in my veins as I slumber?

The Torrent

It's always changing, her
face, how it shifts in the dark, how
I watch it turn, I yearn. (I burn)
Blood simmering, stitching below the surface, enchanted
Upon every twist and shout of the soul. No,

Nose dissolving, chins doubling down, this
Is how it all falls out, this
Is the rain that came and brained me, but
her eyes, a sparkling hue of emerald they
never change, not one inch of them from me, just…a grid. It's

An endless place of possibilities
Starting from my fingertips, weightless
Lines that spin outwards, rushing up then over, graze
Space between wall and floor, mount
Upwards to the rooftops, these prayers, the failing.

Perhaps if I were to climb a tower,
Gaze out upon all the long lands between here & lakeside shore, I
Could see starshine mounting, witness the rivulets and how
Everything is and how and could should be; move
the treetops aside, the roofs fall apart, my mind

Crackles there too as I lose her, myself, a fall against the wall, it
Resembles some large animal scurrying through the underbrush, it
Parts the very treetops aside, I (oh god)
Do her eyes match her soul, unwavering? Am I
going to ruin it once again?

Speak then, say this prayer for the broken refugee.

It's an Expanding Ball Most Easy First to Swallow

Tonight, I play this evil Santa;
fly through the night on a steed of pure steel,
across dusty moors & melting snow.
For the deliverance of two cards, love;
in the other, a second wolf named omittance.

I will not allow myself
tonight, to be driven by desire.
One can create a quite night,
with bullets or hellfire second:
my first choice again is love.

Love that does speak its name
each night, at nine-thirty,
reminding me we could always be.
Something more in store for the cutter,
the man who flies in a chariot with windows down.

Thinking of frozen motion, while the wind nips.

I felt a forearm once, felt the bone quiver beneath,
setting my heart in motion, in fear
fear that I could once again fall for a supple frame,
breasts that could quiet even this still night air;
make me listen to just the sound of breathing.

Watch the exhale as a crafted smoke,
knowing that cold and heat meet to provide fug;
a misty sound that invades her navel.
I've never known how to love that artist,
yet always craft on every day myself.

It's why one card remains now in mailbox,
the other is destined for the waste bin.
Burn their slowly chariot; my own time nears.

Tales

Glass rose, not an enchantment for noses;
you're a gilded tome for the woe-filled tale,
open only with a converse tickle.

Be worthy of my siren song to sing.

I knew a Gnome, entangled in your folds,
one who scurried with each new birth of day
away from the hurries of the light, but soft
what distant beastly noises did she flee?
Not creatures, trolls, or others that make sound.
No. It was the subtleties that dawn brings:

Dry glow, diamond dew; the halo mounting
'round the Son I pray to with each passing.
She was beautiful, no less than darkness
falling fast, ensnaring toes first, then heart
held to the last. Playful rouse then to rest.
I know her only by your hanging, rose.

Lost her no less where the trail-head foundered.
Yet every eve to take the silent guard,
strike out amongst the briar patch that grows;
follow that sing song drifting through the boughs.
Search wearily till the daybreak blossoms,
again somewhere beyond the twilight fauns.

Tome, hold me close with lips that press to sip;
take this breath, let each petal drift & flow,
released upon a pinna found most worthy.
Grow upon that breast, where my longing ends.

Thin Lizzy

Oh dearest Liz, my tizzy missy be:
Where forth did your tin frame and time escape to? I
despair without your simple guidance, collapse beside
Your stout appearance & a failure for what I truly ended up being, I

You…

The way in which ya twirl your hair, the oils collecting there, can
it rebuild me-hold each lock by which remembered too?
Could it right this crumpled mastodon trumpeting angrily,
(bring cold blood to Siberian flesh), or push me perspiration?
I climb this hill to see myself, your shadow long there, I alone
Like a cobweb catching sun, twinkling in the dew
Enshrouded by fell light; a November gale withering.

So you.

When first I entered your supple embrace, it was
with small questioning smiles, a wink beside a nod
Eggnog and a look in which you broke me.

When by practice I learned your routine, your
Contortions and momentary pausure, I
Ascended to new heights, any simple delights,
Released my soul deeply into your hopeful void, a crevice
Turning your lower torso into, toward my passion,
Sensing feet, joints
All the parts that make an aging woman.

You left me for a skeletal form, born
Of which I can only remember shades of you now, so
By the light of your shower curtain flew I knew
The way my chin rested on your forehead, tested
When hugging flavor upset happy, the color of my chest best
I leave you now; a naked figure in a shower strung there, forlorn.

My dear city most foul upon the mountainside held, there
As a figure comes to me on mud feet held, meld
Too easy for me to read its first glance tales wail your hate for
The soft stance of a glance of the way I need to see you, believe
Its soft lips pressed squarely on my forehead, grieved dearly…

My brains leaking for the governed man to follow, swallow words
"Here!" it cries, "Hear here!" until my dear one goes, passes.
A whisk of tuberculosis, whiskey dreaming flailing & it is gone.
Priding itself on countersurveillance evidence piling high, gone
like so many droplets between drug hits, boughs drooping
Winding away through an enchanted syllabus my mind it whittles,
Settles there: adieu.

Footsteps?

I do not know what strength lies in my blood, but
empower me as you can sweet light and
I shall swing that hammer thus again.
Break that mountain blow by blow, until
these hands begin to bleed, until
these bones decide to crack, until
work and conscience become but as one.

Spider as I am, trapped here in a fisherman's net.

Parchment

Found a book today, a
tome of all the girls, of
souls that wandered through a common life took
thus and mine away.

Ticker tape self for a mans strife, he
sounds as such a drag, they
carving up through this whole world, a
blade of loving company, thus untouchable. For

I've my own plans, have sealed this tome of hope, sent it
to you dear ma-ma, dear drip drop slingers all of stone
As perhaps you'd be better understood, me
I don't.

Patience thus held, patience
now aptly learned, enough

yoga and soda to satisfy us all, this
'greatness' like trivialities & uselessness is wearing thin,
boils upon this mask of life so
.

Burn baby burn – may it thus
stain our hands so deeply, utterly.

Completely.

Memory

That crazy/beautiful thing, she
Deserving of a smile I
wanted once to ask her
out to run and jump and date
Skip around the play,
(Couldn't remain the same)
Not even as a pinky finger swells there?

Forgetful.

Sad lover for whom I took it slow
Shook hate and ran slow away now.
(She'll never get to see the sun anyhow)
Somehow forgot to smile the
way that she simply fails,
Da way she slips to fall,
Shot for the stars;
I collapsed then, anywhere, anyway

So
Said lover, take it fine
I've got to get her off my mind.
Cut the wound too deep to bleed now,
(Music as the only balm to rouse now)
Think about me any day now.
Still in love, but I'm missing her
Always on my mind.

Said lover, take it slow
Carve it off my mind.
All I need is just a little hate now,
Something that'll make me feel fine

Said lover, take me now
Come on lets go inside.
She trembled my heart, and took a little patience
(All I've got is this hated)
All I need is just a bit of cotics-narco, so

Now you are here, all against the night.
My sweet Cosette, should I take flight.
Live in peace, then now and forever?
This life forever cursed
(By hand of fate, or something worse?)
Bid me now forever jump, if only just to survive.
(Or bid me final, a wish to die.)
Into darkness, we now go
Down long corridors, past many begotten rooms
Metal triumphs of all the rage

Rudeness fool, dance upon the roof of life.

Antennas; sometimes on my mind
(I can feel the moon rise)
Like the changes of the air,
The starshine, so bright here, there, anywhere
Till I realize it's the glow of love,
(A cry from up above)
Forever etched upon your eyes, so

Don't bend mine, and I wont bend yours
Twist us into shape
To say those simple words, put meaning to their worth
Till the world burns, I yearn again and again
And watch those filaments twirl again.
Ill hold you there, just to keep them strait.
Nibble on your hair.
Its soft. Like you. Tweeewewwe.

What Do you Know of Paradise?

I relied on a human girl,
To keep the fractured pieces of my soul
Tucked neat in a jam jar by the windowsill,
Opened with trembling hands,
The kind that work best for holding.
It is a type of foolishness
That can only be gauged
By the type of wire one dangles by
Or a silhouette of bloody gums
Of frozen tongues in what was once,
The wasteland of my life
As the starshine lightens the western sky,
I look up and question
Why my eyes begin to falter.

I walked the world today, and did not know I sinned.
I saw the world, the world replied in kind,
Yet I know I did not sin.

This they yelled at me, scolded; they even begged me to believe.
Yet still I skip along with frilly flip flops and know better: they lie.

The preacher man looked down upon me,
While I was on my knees
Because he had the men build his pulpit tall, that's all.

I don't know what is in it for him but sin,
But I know, not lordship; only "good lord".
This I know

If no one around me said I sinned, then I could not
If I didn't believe that wretched we see,
Indeed I would not be.

Somehow, as I pen these words I am free
And that is all I need.

The Letter D

Drunk he stopped by and with that she took him,
The fuzzy couch then held their love, jaguar print falls
That floor somehow next gained their frame;
The wall somewhere by the door withstood it all.

That night, I beheld a book, a garbled thing,
lost in so many characters ruined
Whilst she called to me out the open window
Told me of a pain, of a trouble left to soothe

I held quick in recourse, fast to understand,
Hinted at an abdominal issue,
Insisted I come hither, fakery close at hand.
This story, it is mine made, ignore enough to shake it.

So she made him spaghetti in the morning,
Tried in vain to hold his hand
Put orange juice on the noodles,
White digits resist the laugh.

And gone, quickly gone
Back out the same door slammed
He saw quickly through the rouse, how
Neatly she made the plan.

No here I lay, wondering at the moment
Of a girl that once mine; I do not know the flavor
Of wanting to share that passion make
(Oh to take them both?)

The failure that was open mind, uneasy yet to be,
And wonder now at wanders, simply not to be.

...This is What Happens When I Throw You Against the Floorboards

A groaning sound forlorn,
A whisper in rooms choked by thin walls,
Flimsy drywall lit with dying glow; city glow.

How my heart folds upon the first embrace.

Your libido is something I enjoy discarding,
While this room a frame against
Which your body and bent knees are silhouetted,
Smiling. Sleepless I recoil,
cling to the baseboard from just her touch.

A girl, by any other name and time would not smell,
Like earth and oil – lips against fingertips,
A coffee smell against soft crotch
And tongue between my teeth.
Heartbeat from dew soaked wrists.
This is she; this is our passion.
And sometimes, a soul is allowed to come back,
And it only has this single year in which to redeem itself.

Star Gazer

There is a small capsule; silver rim tipped that will
nab that small child while he is out a wanderin (he there a walking)
zipping home, skipping small stones, a whistling, smiling on
at near horizon, unsuspecting; something which has come down

out thirty miles of nimbus now to drown him, somehow claim him.

A cloud chaser: it will pluck him from this earth then cartwheel
forgotten, traveling to the dividing line of night, turning there in
a promise held; a mother's hug withheld out of dear hate, per
ception spins out thus slowly, out then to farthest shore of sight.

Reflected in the widening eyes he yells now, countless
points of light becoming an endless sunrise, futile
frosted drippage whizzing high, crystalize so slowly, caught as
sparkle upon a snowflake, leaking from his retina he weeps.

(So soundless as to never catch as whisper)
So desiring a sonnet, with tongue flex to react in spoken words, or
musing hidden thought; those have become something more, dear
not I, utmost Mercutio, or dripping placental vibe, not I calling

new crags birthing on the rim of prose, not I
crafted wet; mountains of nimbus then to fracture.
What will he return as?
An old man greeting me one day(?), he

colder now, bolder now
said my son's childhood name, he
Pales enough to wake in paradise, he dreams, he
shakes.

He is a drunk wandering the Thames at midnight, I just
a listless form with a wagging tongue, horse smell muttering
up to himself how he hears imagined bells, yelling now, signaling
wavering up to open sky; the air somehow thus replies.

Wondering which larva will hatch, which Lie will hold for now
(she has been waiting, watching so, utterly brisk, patiently silver)

Glow milking the last day fade color, burning out
there on the western edge of terra firma, gloats
Floats up there then to meet us.
(Or gutter pasture, holding you so long, yes as)

Father sky pours out his gourd filling fast, lets
flowers blossom upon the open chest,
(Breeze fed, liquid caught; droplets stuck in sand so near)
May it be enough to claim he, me, we (us. them.)

To My Mother

The woman who mattered most,
I hold your hand.
To the girl who cried my name, held my tears
The one most easily discarded,
The one who watch me grow,
The one I sometimes hated.
To her I now go.

The 50's dreams are dying,
The 80's demagogues who sought to hoard it all,
Will we outlast them?
Better: will we outlast ourselves?

This poem goes out to her, for her.
Her who fucked the most.
Suicide by patient fire,
A mental burning at once held
Whilst doth I carved my name on another,

If only to forget her face.
If only to escape a name
It is trouble to remember her,
Trouble now which follows,
A tunnel
Eclipse of a life,
At one, once, and almost broken.

To sit, without stirring
Stringed instruments abound
I kept checking the letter box,
In expectation of something coming,
Never sure what it was to be
Was more than satisfied with the result,

She was the one with too large pencil,
I can see her when she was five,
Same precise mood, same driven prose,
A continued feisty attitude, with bangs in her eyes
Bangs in her eyes,
The same driven
I cannot believe she can drive it out,
One drunk night to erase my existence.

Can it be so easy?

'delphia

Oh you, read this tome you oh crazy thing & ton & on the
rainy days (or else on so many drugs), or out along the
many sad nights as your eyes dry, weeping not, falling not
no more so fast as the Son rises high, nor upon I, I all, really

all the lies you wasted on, oh no I weep, I fall, you wail as I
thus call out to the many memories you do your best to forget, I
dying not necessarily just for a try, or (no) not to...forget? Not, no

slinking into the lingering night, not passed diamond stores or
Historical markers that at once remind, that something
important happened in this town; once hearts did uplift & I
in that moment knew the shame, wandered away without a name. I

you will guess that one inkling, I
A failing organ fast to pump, I
Of a heart so full at a passing pissing hate, I
Despair not of a city growing (or) Midtown rise, I sit alone & think

It rises.

Yes I saw your loving frame there, yes you walked & screamed & I
Hated (not danced) along all these empty city streets, I opened up;
attempted to explain to others all the things we loved all at once I
Think there was a large bath there, ringed not with guts but MOLD

With petrol or wood flame, or all the things a man can collect in a
lifetime piled high, cinders stand beside (one hand rises); chance?
You grew there for a little while (shadows falling over) a match?

Yet I know enough to say I don't know you, not your signing, nor
The now or the how or the why of clouds calling, nor
the love that surrounds our veins, cutting into a sane brain; nor
The way your name treads lightly on tongue forlorn. (His?)

You just left, never really gave a reason why, just left, never
Spoke to the darkness or my friends, just left.

This is to her; it is a shifting of planets gathering fast,
The many miles to heaven parting, we fall, meanwhile
I had dropped my simple foolishness, merely Ignored
being glad to gain a grin I'd still have her.

Saved for the sky is falling.

I felt enough 2 light flame, not bones-fired, or the many ways 2 get
Away from the shame I felt in calling of you, you drip a lot, consider
Ably free enough to feel shame and for that remorseless stupid I
Witness only as others can do. I left, I wept again.

Philos

For I felt it, smelt it, dwell on supple thoughts too: caught upon her
green gaze the children we never had to rise there, the black hair
Ravens mane all; the tillandsia growing in small clumps, all the
the subtle ways she packs her things (she says she's leaving), the
lungs catch on fast wire strung out in air I saw not fibres nor…

It was her wrists, her frame: in them she remains as beautiful, a
moment, my frame - da long days before I throw those too away, a
Mound pointing in all the right directions, dark parking of the lips, a
of darkened twisted straggles, shifting of her hips as day breaks.

I fall asleep or else in love again. BUT!

send the love and the feels out to the wayward sand, no need
for travel; only to close all the doors behind her, forgetting that
one day a thief of expert care with short shall stand beside, not I…
The first time I broke on a long shot, not long before eyes fail, I

I yes yet I, I still have them in my windpipe drainpipe.
And in that small maze, we broke, saw visions we
were aloud to love and fleet again we &
me floundering in fast surf, drowning out there again. So now. Now

I wish now that we'd opp'sed back then – bred
all this new sickness into a newer, gooder type of family, a
Simile that smiles on as the water gathers then recedes, hair
Gathers to proceed (witness to concede)…

The phone cords cut, the thus reception dies, long miles become
Friendly only to spinning wheels or passing wind, I hate cuz that
Briefcase full of Chinese knickknacks collects dust, destined
for a shattering of long days, & truthful glances under thick sun, t

tall then, philos thus feel it (shape it teal, take the better part of the)
color of your trial, the bending of bones, (I wont be there) yes,
This tome it remains uncompleted, just like the falling of you
I upon Kepler tombstones, you roaring up, loudly, fast -

I still remain there, and
For in these words, we break

and yet begin again…

Maybe in some faraway place I will find you
(And be allowed to take you home)
or at least, hold your gaze but a little awhile
your hand, one last time, to remember what its like to hear you
speak my name
three syllables spoken softly, thus please, add on..

i wish i could remember what it was like to hold you close
because, you probably have watched a hundred times from your
lofty cloud, as i've held a blade in your stead
and watched a hundred more in your own silent prayer as i
replaced its gentle gleam yet to unfold
it once again, while whispering my own quiet reminders that

i suppose i should have always known, that i could fall for blonde
hair and blue eyes for reckless hate, and
fear that comes from a sadistic smile
exchanges help, however, and keep us alive: human once again
(if only for a little while)

you once asked me to make that final change.

while you sit and cry in joyful love, i will show how much a
forgotten face can still mean
i will give up forever, if just to touch you softly
with only the back of my hand, while you however, only gave up a
simple body for a simpler boy
and now, i will give it all away, to carry your memories up to the
very sky

take me for one last dance, cold friend
and tell me how much regret, and sweetness, and sadness can all
partake here in this single moment; a

lost artist with the ability to create no more

This set of poetry is a (my) search for (and amongst) women,
2007-2017, and oh how it is filled with stumbles, grumbles, all.
      (may it be a reminder of a better times) & expeditions
      thus Worthy to mount!

This piece is also dedicated to the heart; for the lady (ladies?) that
are and never yet could never be. The one that doesn't break or
flake...rises in the dark only to shine, oh thus so shine upon
(...thus truly the one that would never, ever be right for me.)

I see!
We made it, and thus in time grew
In spirit and in depth
Love as much as breadth, and in
Such consideration were shown, allowed
To be something more.

(Thus pulled us all then through time & space, & so a thank you..)

So for now, we rest, wondering at the movements, the muses that
shape us all.

From the utter bottom of my (our) hearts..
Thank.

                You.

"In lovers' hearts summer goes on
And no sad leaves descend upon
A resigned earth – our game's still playing
Each kiss is worth a sunlit day'
        -Peter Gordon, 1999 (www.aloveinverse.com)
        (A man who wrote his wife a poem a day for 25 years)

"So, sha la, la, la, la, my lady
   Now every mile away (and every day)
      Cuts a little bit deeper..."
         -Jay Ferguson ("Thunder Island", 1977)

here is the deepest secret nobody knows
(here is the root of the root and the bud of the bud
and the sky of the sky of a tree call life; which
grows
higher than soul can hope or mind can hide)
and this is the wonder that's keeping the stars apart

i carry your heart (I carry it in my heart)

-e.e. cummings
("I Carry your Heart With Me", 1952)

www.ingramcontent.com/pod-product-compliance
Lightning Source LLC
Chambersburg PA
CBHW060346050426
42449CB00011B/2848